Modern information technologies for web applications

Badral Baigaltugs

Modern information technologies for web applications

LAP LAMBERT Academic Publishing

Impressum / Imprint

Bibliografische Information der Deutschen Nationalbibliothek: Die Deutsche Nationalbibliothek verzeichnet diese Publikation in der Deutschen Nationalbibliografie; detaillierte bibliografische Daten sind im Internet über http://dnb.d-nb.de abrufbar.

Alle in diesem Buch genannten Marken und Produktnamen unterliegen warenzeichen-, marken- oder patentrechtlichem Schutz bzw. sind Warenzeichen oder eingetragene Warenzeichen der jeweiligen Inhaber. Die Wiedergabe von Marken, Produktnamen, Gebrauchsnamen, Handelsnamen, Warenbezeichnungen u.s.w. in diesem Werk berechtigt auch ohne besondere Kennzeichnung nicht zu der Annahme, dass solche Namen im Sinne der Warenzeichen- und Markenschutzgesetzgebung als frei zu betrachten wären und daher von jedermann benutzt werden dürften.

Bibliographic information published by the Deutsche Nationalbibliothek: The Deutsche Nationalbibliothek lists this publication in the Deutsche Nationalbibliografie; detailed bibliographic data are available in the Internet at http://dnb.d-nb.de.

Any brand names and product names mentioned in this book are subject to trademark, brand or patent protection and are trademarks or registered trademarks of their respective holders. The use of brand names, product names, common names, trade names, product descriptions etc. even without a particular marking in this works is in no way to be construed to mean that such names may be regarded as unrestricted in respect of trademark and brand protection legislation and could thus be used by anyone.

Coverbild / Cover image: www.ingimage.com

Verlag / Publisher:
LAP LAMBERT Academic Publishing
ist ein Imprint der / is a trademark of
OmniScriptum GmbH & Co. KG
Heinrich-Böcking-Str. 6-8, 66121 Saarbrücken, Deutschland / Germany
Email: info@lap-publishing.com

Herstellung: siehe letzte Seite /
Printed at: see last page
ISBN: 978-3-659-52830-9

Modern Information Technologies for Web Applications

Acknowledgement

I would like to thank Ing. Miloš Ulman Ph.D, for his advice and supervision of my diploma thesis. Also I would like to show my gratitude to my colleagues and friends Mr. Raphael Kwaku Botchway and Mr. Tuan Minh Tran who supported me and shared their information throughout the period of my research and development work.

Modern Information Technologies for Web Applications

Summary

In modern days web applications are occupying the largest space in everyday life of the people. Throughout the years, the active web applications have been increasing tremendously. Due to the enhancement of the web world the techniques building those web sites are also changing rapidly. And this thesis deals with the issues regarding to the modern technologies for the web application development.

The thesis has three main sections in it which are dealing with the modern information technologies for the web application on behalf of the theoretical and practical views. In the first section of the thesis it depicts the research and study of the web technologies. The second section covers the full practical view which includes designing and implementing the particular web application system with chosen platform. Within this designing and implementing part it has detailed specifications of data gathering process, database designing and finally application programming.

And the third section includes the analytical comparison of the developed application which is made in the previous section with another web application that having same processes but built in a different technology. Comparison process has been implemented on the basis of technical features from both application systems and these features are described in detail.

Keywords

Software development, web application, e-commerce, online meeting, online schedule, human software organization, financial resource management

Table of Contents

1.   Introduction

For the last decades the usage of the Internet has been growing rapidly in worldwide. From the middle of 90's the websites popularity had taken place effectively and now almost each organization, company and even individuals have their own websites (or simply web pages) to represent their activities, interests and hobbies. Following this procedure there are variety of technologies created by different inventors and software developers from all over the countries.

There are many web application frameworks had been invented which facilitate rapid application development. At the early time the basic web language was established which known as Hyper Text Markup Language (HTML). Following the spread utilization of the HTML the newest technologies based on HTML has arisen in the recent years. The main advantage that the technologies give to the users and makes it popular is its compatibility of cross-platform. Modern web application technologies have several types of benefits. The first one is that it can be performed independently from any operating system. If we take a look at some technology frameworks such as Ruby on Rails, Python, PHP or Perl, those could be used to develop any web application by the software developers on any platform. The next significant point is that using modern technologies developers are capable to create multi-functional web applications with multi-threading process handling. For instance, there are some application online retail sales which include webmail and online auctions at the same time. In addition, modern technologies can be divided into particular categories according to what kind of web system it is used to. There is a common technology that is comfortable for creating Intranets which are mainly used for the internal activities in a company. And there are technologies for creating Social Networking Services, Online auctions and other multi-usage web applications.

Nowadays private companies, government organizations have their own software developers who are responsible to create the web application and maintain it for every day's internal activities in the organization. And in many cases those responsibilities face the problem for choosing the proper technology that affordable for their work and this thesis could offer the most possible technologies by explaining and demonstrating the solutions which made with the given particular example application.

2. Objectives and Methodology

2.1. Objectives

In diploma thesis the modern technologies for developing web applications are covered with the example of a particular technology. In the first part of objective, it contains the information for researching and studying the requirements which will be used for the new application system.

The second part of the objective contains the demonstration of the process and the final outcome of the application development. Regarding to the system, the web application is considered as the common software (such as electronic office or social networking service) which could be adapted for everyday activities in the company or other organizations. The technology for developing the web system was chosen according to the author's own choice of evaluating the platform tools for the web application. The core idea of the second objective part is to demonstrate the advantages by highlighting the particular features of the using technology for the web application development.

In the last and the third part of the objective contains the comparison of the known technology tools. One of the technologies is the platform which has used to develop the web application. The comparison analysis is made in terms of web application technology having same purposes but built on various technologies by emphasizing their diversities.

2.2.   Methodology

The methodology of the thesis is based on research of relevant information resources. Practical process will be derived from results which will be given by the research study. Finally, comparison of analysis of the system with another similar systems made in a different development platform will be made. Based on the synthesis of the theoretical and the practical knowledge, final conclusions will be formulated.

The several methodology parts are defined to accomplish the thesis. In the first part collected the necessary information about the web application. Also the information about the variety web applications is collected roundly. The further step was to define requirements of the application in order to exactly characterize the system processes. Within this requirements the definitions, the tables and the graphs are also fulfilled due to properly do the practical section of the thesis. Based on specified requirements at the previous step the workflows and detailed structures of developing application are made.

The next part is to develop the targeting web application. This process is fulfilled based on analyzing the specifications concluded in the previous research and study. After the development of the system the comparison between the two similar systems built on different technologies is done. The comparison part is expressed by analyzing certain kind of software technology features which have mutually covered in both different technologies. Finally formulation of the conclusions is expressly made with the basis on theoretical and practical knowledge gathered in the diploma thesis.

3. Motivation

This chapter discusses about the situations of the web development technologies in broad way and its challenges that might be facing currently.

3.1. Problem Definition

In the early web development generations during the mid-90s the main issues of web technologies were basically concentrated on how to comfortably build-up the contents which could be attached in the internal body of the web development. This was called the way of static development which is commonly familiar with the ordinary customers and it diversifies from the way of dynamic development with the usage of database technologies, various tools and other accessories. As for the new technologies emerging in the present days, the worry about issue has been shifting from content based development to effectively rapid development. It can be recognized as how simply the design pattern is organized and either this is consistently flexible or not for those who maintain the application. If we take a look at the oldest, widely used technologies particularly Java, PHP or ASP, unlike modern technologies, their codes in the structure are scattered throughout the bone structure of HTML which prevents the development progress from fasten up.

3.2. Problem Solution

The clients who claim to use the web application not only want safe applications but want to use those applications when they have completed in a short time and it makes customers to feel that the application they use is life-long stable and potentially safe as well.

10

The latest open web technologies like Django, Python and Ruby on Rails have shown dramatic changes in terms of approaching easy-way coding, time saving development. These features make them to consider as possible solutions for developing web applications which the customers willingly accept to use. The issue which occurs in the case of customers is similar to the case of business organizations (company, corporations and other non-government organizations). The companies and organizations wish to protect their data from the outside and believe that the internal day-to-day process must be equally distributed to all its employees that they can contribute to it as much as effectively. Due to this reason, the organizations have vital needs to use a complex interactive system such as CMS (Content Management System) system and other types of similar platforms. In this thesis Ruby on Rails technology will be the main platform that tries to solve the above mentioned problems and the main application to demonstrate will be the particular complete module of CMS system.

4. Literature Review

This chapter discusses the main findings revealed from the reviewed articles and other publishes. Firstly the understanding of the Web application along with particular historical perspectives is widely presented in the top part of the chapter. The chapter continues with the common architecture and internal designs of the web applications.

4.1. Comprehending the Web Application

From the technical point of view, the web application can be defined as highly programmable environment which utilizes web and web browser technology to fulfill one or more than one tasks through network. On the other hand Web application is something more than just a 'Web site'. Web Application is a client/server application that uses a Web browser as its client program, and performs and interactive service through connecting with servers over the Internet (or Intranet). A Web site simply delivers content from static files. A Web application presents dynamically tailored content based on request parameters, tracked user behaviors, and security considerations.

The historical perspectives with fundamental information can help to approach more closely understanding the Web application.

TCP/IP

The original fruit was the ARPANET. TCP/IP Protocol Suite has been evolved into its current form starting behind the protocols of ARPANET for over time. TCP/IP refers to two of the most important protocols within the suite: TCP (Transmission Control Protocol) and IP (Internet Protocol)

Layers

TCP/IP associated protocol layers are:

1. The *Network Interface (Network Access)* Layer

2. The *Internet* Layer

3. The *Transport* Layer

4. The *Application* Layer

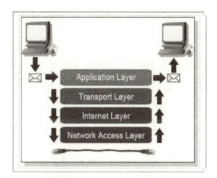

Figure 4.1: TCP/IP Layer message transmission process

Source: http://learn-networking.com

Because of protocol taxonomy contains layers, these protocols are often known as a *protocol stack*.

13

The authors Shklar & Rozen (2003) mentioned about some of the common technologies in their book:

The **Network Interface layer** is the layer responsible for the lowest level of data transmission within TCP/IP, facilitating communication with the underlying physical network.

The **Internet layer** provides the mechanisms for intersystem communications, controlling message routing, validity checking, and message header composition/decomposition. The protocol known as IP (which stands, oddly enough, for Internet Protocol) operates on this layer, as does ICMP (the Internet Control Message Protocol). ICMP handles the transmission of control and error messages between systems. Ping is an Internet service that operates through ICMP.

The **Transport layer** provides message transport services between applications running on remote systems. This is the layer in which TCP (the Transmission Control Protocol) operates. TCP provides reliable, connection-oriented message transport.

The **Application layer** is the highest level within the TCP/IP protocol stack. It is within this layer that most of the services we associate with 'the Internet' operate.

There are common TCP/IP application services including Telnet, E-mail (electronic mail), message forums, live messaging, and file servers.

1. **Telnet** – It operates with the Application layer. Telnet used command-line interface in order to log in remotely to other system that were accessible over the Internet.

2. **E-mail** – It exchanges text information between the people or communities via TCP/IP service. The transmission of electronic mail is performed through the SMTP protocols. The reading of electronic mail is usually through either POP or IMAP.

3. **Message forums** - Message forums are online services that allow users to write messages to be posted on the electronic bulletin board, and to read similar messages that others have posted. These messages are usually organized into categories so that people can find the kinds of messages they are looking for.

14

4. **Live messaging** - America Online Instant Messaging service may be responsible for making the notion of IM-ing someone part of our collective vocabulary. Long before the existence of AOL, there was a talk protocol that enabled users logged in to network-connected UNIX systems to talk to each other. A talk server would run on a UNIX machine, waiting for requests from other talk servers. (Since talk was a bi-directional service, servers had to run on the machines at both ends of a conversation.) A user would invoke the talk client program to communicate with a person on another machine somewhere else on the network, e.g. patrick@graceland.org . Today the vast majority of Internet users communicate each other every minute via well-known user interfaced IMs such as Yahoo Messenger, Google Talk. The first Internet chat software in widespread use, Internet Relay Chat (IRC), provided both public and private chat facilities.

5. **File Servers** - providing remote access to more persistent documents and files is a fundamental necessity to enable sharing of resources. For years before the existence of the Internet, files were shared using BBS 's (electronic Bulletin Board Systems). Users would dial in to a BBS via a modem, and once it connected, they would able to access to directories of files to download. Various file transfer protocols were used to enable this functionality over telephone dialup lines (e.g. Kermit, Xmodem, Zmodem). To facilitate this functionality over the Internet, the File Transfer Protocol (FTP) was created (Shklar & Rosen. 2003).

WWW (World Wide Web)

The World Wide Web was developed in the early 1990s. The system he proposed has propagated itself into what can truly be called a World Wide Web, as people all over the world use it for a wide variety of purposes.

To understand why the Web supplanted the other technologies, it will be helpful to know a bit about the mechanics of the Web and other Internet information management technologies. All

15

of these technologies consist of (at least) two types of software: server and client. An Internet-connected computer that wishes to provide information to other Internet systems must run server software, and a system that wishes to access the information provided by servers must run client software (for the Web, the client software is normally a web browser). The server and client applications communicate over the Internet by following a communication protocol built on top of TCP/IP (Shklar & Rosen. 2003).

Web sites to Web application

Shklar & Rozen (2003) briefly written about what was the steps of the web sites turning into web applications or becoming a part of the web applications.

When the Web site is being provided by dynamic information services as well as it's supported by the connection to relational database, now it considered as the real Web application. As for the content, the requirement of the contents will not be limited as a static, but fully compatible with the database in which the contents are stored, accessed to and permanently modified.

Web applications must understand not only HTTP and HTML, but the other underlying Internet protocols as well. They must be familiar with JavaScript, XML, relational databases, graphic design and multimedia. They must be well versed in application server technology, and have a strong background in information architecture.

16

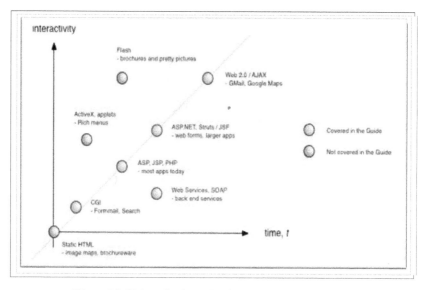

Figure 4.2: Web application technologies through the time period

The key principle that makes today's web applications so popular, as are inheritable which supports for cross-platform compatibility is the ability to maintain and upgrade them without changing and re-installing software itself on client computers located in different continents. Without these particular features, there would be no social networking services like Facebook, Google+, blogs, online retailing system, internet banking and no blogs, no web forum communications.

For all web applications the architecture of the internal structure are basically similar which broken into logical concept of "tiers" or multi-tier architecture. The most widespread usage of the tier architecture is 3-tier architecture. This 3-tier architecture diversifies from the previous architecture mainframe (1-tier) and client-server (2-tier).

17

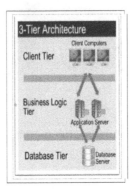

Figure 4.3: The basic structure of 3-tier architecture

Source: http://www.simcrest.com

3-tier architecture consists of the following tiers (Lane & Williams. 2004):

- **Presentation tier** – This is the highest level of the application where displays the data information on the browser. It communicates with other tier through displaying output results to the browser.

- **Application tier** (sometimes called business logic tier) – This is the tier logically located in the mid of the architecture where handles all functionalities and other detailed processes of the application. It could be either computer processors or application servers.

- **Data tier** – Database servers are considered as this tier where data is stored and retrieved. It keeps data separately from other two tiers and communicates only with the application tier in order to store and retrieve data.

Web applications are generally classified into main three types in terms of how they interact with the customers. However this classification cannot apply for all applications like Google mail, but it can fully represent the main types of applications.

- **Customer-facing** applications are better known as e-commerce or Business2Client sites. These sites offer services and products to customers to buy with payment card and shopping cart.

- **Employee-facing** applications are known as intranet sites which commonly used in a company. The largest and the complex applications are ERP (Enterprise Resource Planning) system or CRM (Customer Relationship Management) system. In the previous these applications were operated on internal client-server network. Now they are web-enabled and are made easy to deploy by providing the usage of XML and web services.

- **Customer-Supplier facing** applications are better known as Business2Business and it uses extranet which is an extensible of the intranet. It allows companies to share their project management and development progress of the product with other outside companies (Lane & Williams. 2004).

When using web applications there are certain seemingly benefits and drawbacks the application maintainers or ordinary users could experience. The benefits are listed at the following:

- No required configurations on client computers needed. Web applications allow saving spaces on the client by requiring the space only for browser/navigator software.

- Provide cross-platform compatibility – Web applications are easily transform in different operation systems

- Accessible from anywhere in the world through Internet connection

- Secure and easy backup centralized data store

- Available for 24 hours and 7 days

And the disadvantages are:

- More dependent on internet connection. May cause slow run of web application

- Development process could take longer time

- Certain risks are still exist in secure operation

4.2. Web Application Architecture Principles

Firstly, modern Web application development frameworks are based on the OOP (Object-Oriented Programming) which is the main fundamental idea for the comfortable software programming. Behind the OOP idea it's hidden the cognitive models to solve the problems. Object oriented systems more closely resemble our cognitive models and visual models drawn from them. A fundamental reason for using the object oriented programming is that it narrows the semantic gap between the problem we think in natural way and the way we work with them on a computer.

Web application frameworks aim to achieve that fleeting goal of good Web application architecture — separation of content from presentation — by making developers responsible for program logic and access to content, while giving creative page designers control over presentation formatting. Ideally, these distinct functions should reside in separate source objects, so that designers and developers do not 'collide' with each other while doing their respective jobs.

The spectrum of Web application approaches are widely described by Shklar & Rozen (2003). Web applications can be divided into four broad categories:

1. Scripting or programmatic approaches,

2. Template approaches,

3. Hybrid approaches, and

4. Frameworks.

Programmatic Approaches

In scripting or programmatic approaches, the source associated with the page object consists predominantly of code written in Perl, Python, or a high-level programming language like Java. The code may be interspersed with some degree of formatting constructs. Naturally, such approaches appeal to programmers. The bulk of the page object consists of application logic, while the page formatting (e.g. HTML) is generally produced using output statements in the associated programming language.

Template Approaches

The template approach uses a source object (the template) that consists pre-dominantly of formatting structures, with limited embedded constructs that add programmatic power. The focus of the source object is on formatting, not programming logic. Naturally, this approach appeals to Web page authors and graphic designers much more than the scripting/programmatic approach.

Hybrid Approaches

This approaches combine scripting elements with template structures. They have more programmatic power than pure templates because they allow embedded blocks containing 'scripts'. It seems to offer the benefit of a page-oriented structure combined with additional programmatic power. Examples of this approach include PHP, Microsoft's Active Server Pages (ASP) and Sun's Java Server Pages (JSP).

Most of the systems have been designed to interpret the hybrid objects into source code. The systems have evolved significantly since their inception, but their origins still expose serious issues with these approaches.

Frameworks

The Frameworks approach technically divided into two groups:

1. MVC (Model-View-Controller) Approaches

2. XML-Based Approaches

MVC (Model-View-Controller) Approaches

In object-oriented terms, this will consist of the set of class which **model** and support the underlying problem, and which therefore, will tend to be stable and as long-lived as the problem itself.

Views are consisting of classes which give us "windows" on the model e.g.

- The GUI/Widget (graphical user interface) view,

- The CLI (command line interface) view,

- The API (Application program interface) view.

Or:

- The novice view,

- The expert view.

A controller is an object that lets you manipulate a view. The controller handles the input while the view handles the output. Controllers have the most knowledge of platforms and

22

operating systems. Views are fairly independent of whether their event comes from Microsoft Windows, or whatever. Controllers were SmallTalk specific. In Java's Swing, for example, the view and controller are combined. In Swing the combined view/controller is called the delegate (Deacon. 2009).

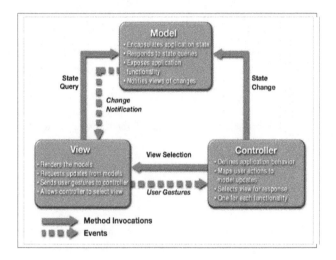

Figure 4.4: MVC Pattern

Source: http://java.sun.com

There are many kinds of web developing frameworks including ASP.NET, CGI, Spring, Yii, CodeIgnite, Symfony and Ruby on Rail. For instance, one model of Sun's Java Server Pages (JSP) JSP Model 2 was the attempt to wrap JSP within the Model-View-Controller paradigm. One of the main advances which came with JSP Model 2 is Sun's specification of the Java Standard Tag Library (JSTL). JSTL specifies the standard set of tags for iteration, conditional processing, database access, and many other formatting functions. The Jakarta project (part of the Apache Software Foundation that gave us the Apache Web Server) includes a subproject that is focusing on JSP taglibs.

The general structure of a Web application using the JSP Model 2 architecture is:

1. User requests are directed to the *controller* servlet.

2. The controller servlet accesses required data and builds the *model*, possibly delegating the processing to helper classes.

3. The controller servlet (or the appropriate subordinate task) selects and passes control to the appropriate JSP responsible for presenting the *view*.

4. The view page is presented to the requesting user.

5. The user interacts with the controller servlet (via the view) to enter and modify data, traverse through results, etc.

XML-based Approaches

In the Web application development a number of approaches uses of XML as the background for their data models. In these approaches, an XML skeleton selected or constructed by the controller module serves as the data model. It may contain request context elements that are exposed to page designers to help them 'flesh out' the skeleton.

There are a few competing XML-based approaches, including another Apache/Jakarta project, Cocoon. None seems robust enough to upset the applecart as a true next generation Web application framework. Nonetheless, this approach has a lot of merit, since XML provides so much flexibility, but there are a number of issues with both existing approaches and with the concept in general.

Application logic and data access should be contained entirely within the controller servlet and its helper classes. The controller servlet should select the appropriate JSP page and transfer control to that page object based on the request parameters, state, and session information.

Name	Approach	Availability	Advantages	Drawbacks
CGI	scripting	open standard	1. Portable across all Web servers. 2. Simple programming paradigm. 3. Modules available to augment base language functionality. 4. Open standard.	1. All HTML formatting performed programmatically. 2. Overhead of process creation and initialization for each request. 3. Programmatic approach puts it beyond grasp of average page designer
SSI	template	open standard	1. Simple syntax. 2. Open standard.	1. Not enough power by today's standards. 2. Security holes.
PHP	scripting	open source	1. Structural change from code focus to page focus. 2. Modules available to augment base language functionality. 3. Open source.	1. Intermixing of code and formatting. 2. Who is the target audience? Page designers? Programmers?

Name	Approach	Availability	Advantages	Drawbacks
Servlet API	scripting	Sun specification (open source implementations available)	1. Portable across all Web servers that support servlets. 2. Access to full power and extensibility of the Java language (JDBC, JNDI, RMI, EJB) 3. Though proprietary, uses open specification with community participation.	1. Programmatic approach puts it beyond grasp of average page designer. 2. HTML formatting still performed programmatically.
Cold Fusion	template/ hybrid	Macromedia proprietary	1. Portable across all Web servers supporting CGI. 2. Simple programming paradigm. 3. Modules available to augment base language functionality. 4. Quick way to get a Web application up and running.	1. Program logic and data access *still* embedded within the page structure. 2. Simpler than most programmatic approaches, but out of reach for most page designers. 3. Proprietary

ASP	hybrid	Microsoft proprietary (has been ported to non-Microsoft environments)	1. Direct access to COM and ActiveX objects, ODBC databases. 2. "Free" (with Microsoft IIS). 3. Quick way to get a Web application up and running.	1. Abrupt intermixing of code and formatting. 2. Visual Basic code orientation not sophisticated and structured enough for advanced scalable Web applications. 3. Too complex for page designers to create without programmer assistance. 4. Proprietary
JSP	hybrid	Sun specification (open source implementations available)	1. Power of servlets within a page-oriented framework. 2. The `<jsp:useBean>` tag allows direct access to named scoped JavaBeans and their accessible properties. 3. Custom taglibs provide extensibility. 4. Though proprietary (like servlets), uses open specification with community participation.	1. Does nothing to prevent or even discourage intermixing of formatting and code. 2. Variable substitution is unnecessarily ornate, and is difficult to read. 3. The claim that JSP is 'accessible' to page designers does not hold up under scrutiny, given the complexity of JSP tags (no improvement over ASP).

Name	Approach	Availability	Advantages	Drawbacks
WebMacro/ Velocity	template	open source	1. True template approach. 2. Limits code infestation within templates to iteration and conditional processing constructs. 3. Works well within MVC architecture.	1. UNIX orientation for parameter substitution—is it friendly/intuitive? 2. Not XML-compliant
Struts	framework	open source	1. Full fledged MVC framework. 2. Infrastructure includes dynamic dispatching, form validation, custom taglibs. 3. Flexibility in selecting presentation views (JSP, Velocity template, etc.).	1. Careful design is required to reap full benefits.
XML-based (e.g. Cocoon)	framework	open source	1. DOM allows encapsulation of all sorts of data. 2. XPath expressions can be used to extract elements (or sets of elements) from the DOM structure. 3. XSLT is a very powerful mechanism for data transformation. 4. Different stylesheets can be established/dynamically pieced together to build pages.	1. Performance of XSLT transformation (even with caching of preprocessed stylesheets) is slow. 2. Complexity of XSLT beyond the grasp of most page designers.

Figure 4.5: Web application development approaches compared

Source: (Shklar & Rozen. 2003)

4.3. Known Web Application Technologies

This sub-chapter will cover the most common used web technologies along their characteristics. Especially this sub chapter highlights the technologies which could be referred to the following general categories:

- Human-readable – The end user who receives the respond from the Web server is exactly human being who is usually using Web browsers submitting HTTP requests. The body of the response is human-readable content such as an HTML page, sound and image.

- Machine-understandable – The recipient is a another Web application rather than human being who is using Web browsers to receive

Also it covers a few of the emerging web services and protocols which provide discrete functionalities for distributed web applications.

Internet technology rapid expansion has come with large cost. Today we are seeing some encouraging examples of technology contingence. XHTML is replacing HTML; WML is started being redefined as an extension to XHTML. The latest specifications from W3C and other standard-defining bodies (for example, OASIS, WAP forum) are concentrating on achieving improvements to emerging technologies. We are heading to the following emerging technologies for distributed web application development:

- **Web Services** – Represents advanced architecture for developing distributed Web applications

27

- **Resource Description Framework** (RDF) – Specification which leads for machine-understandable metadata.

- **XML Query** – Supports retrieving data from XML documents, reduces the gap between Web world and database world.

The term **Web services** means the set of protocols for defining standardized service descriptions, construction, transmission, and process of Web service requests. The popular known protocols and services referring as Web services are:

- SOAP (Simple Object Access Protocol) – Protocol for exchanging structured information based on XML, and it usually relies on Application Layer protocols.

- WSDL (Web Service Description Language) – XML-based language which provides machine-understandable descriptions on how the services work, what kind parameters it does expect and what structure it returns.

- UDDI (Universal Description, Discovery and Integration) – XML-based business registration which is designed to interrogated by SOAP message and provide access to WSDL documents (Shklar & Rosen. 2003).

The **Resource Description Framework** is a standard that was designed to support machine-understandable metadata, and to enable interoperability between metadata-based applications. However XML is used to encode and transport RDF models, it is not an XML application. The most basic RDF concept is that of a resource, which is any entity represented with a URI. An RDF *triple* is the combination of a *subject*, an *object*, and a *property* (Shklar & Rosen. 2003).

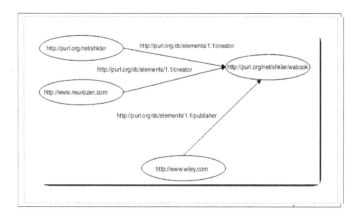

Figure 4.6: Simple RDF model

Source: (Shklar & Rozen. 2003)

The **XML Query** language, XQuery, is still being designed by W3C. There are already numerous implementations based on the early specifications of XML. XQuery combines the notions of query and traversal. The traversal component serves to define the query context, which is determined by the current XML element and its location in the DOM tree. The query component serves to evaluate conditions along different axis (element, attribute, etc.) in the query context. Both components are involved in evaluating an expression (Shklar & Rosen. 2003).

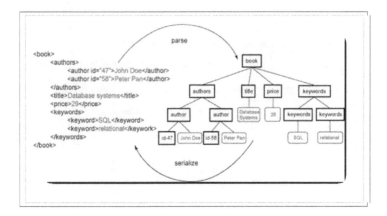

Figure 4.7: Sample XQuery document in textual format and parsed format

Source: http://www.ibm.com

ASP.NET

In Spaanjaars(2010) it is clearly described about the structure of ASP.NET technology. One of the most widely dispersed web application frameworks would be ASP.NET framework. Since its release in 2002 with version 1.0 .NET Framework the technology has been considered as the Web application model which supports the clean coding format. The Web pages of ASP.NET are known as Web Forms which are the main blocks for the web application development. ASP.NET configuration is managed by information stored in XML file (web.config). The codes of ASP.NET are compiled by CLR (Common Language Runtime) which is provided by .NET Framework. This CLR compiles and manages the ASP.NET execution and class.

ASP.NET uses particular design patterns for common problems. Design patterns are used in entire .NET Framework. They are divided into several different types depending on the design problem.

- *Creational Patterns* – Dealt with the best way to create objects. They make a system independent of how the objects are created, represented and composed.

- *Structural Patterns* – Concerned with how classes and objects are composed to form much larger structures. This patterns use an inheritance feature to compose or implement interfaces.

- *Behavioral Patterns* – Concerned algorithms and responsibilities between the objects. It is used composition rather than inheritance (Spaanjaars. 2010, p47).

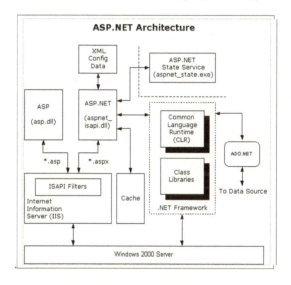

Figure 4.8: ASP.NET development architecture

Source: http://www.directionmicrosoft.com

31

PHP (Hypertext Preprocessor)

PHP is a recursive acronym that stands for PHP: Hypertext Preprocessor; this is in the naming style of GNU, which stands for GNU's Not Unix and which began this odd trend. PHP is a scripting language that's usually embedded or combined with the HTML of a web page. When the page is requested, the web server executes the PHP script and substitutes in the result back into the page. PHP has many excellent libraries that provide fast, customized access to DBMSs and is an ideal tool for developing application logic in the middle tier of a three-tier application (Lane & Williams. 2004).

For a long time, PHP was disregarded as a language not serious enough for rich web applications. In 2007 it has become clear that it has three major web application frameworks extending capabilities of this language: Yii, CodeIgnite, **Symfony, CakePHP**, and **Zend Framework** (Porebski. 2011).

In order to emphasize the components for PHP web application frameworks a particular framework has chosen as Symfony. The further information of the PHP web application will be based on the features of Symfony framework.

As it has mentioned in the previous chapters the structure bone of every modern web application framework stands on Model-View-Controller pattern. As for PHP Symfony framework **controller** is responsible for processing user events. The controllers in Symfony are split into several components.

1. It is the entry point into the application.

2. It determines what action is required to execute.

3. Loads the configurations.

4. Executes the filters.

The **model** represents the applications data and the business rules used to manipulate and access it. Symphony model layer splits into two separate layers: Object Relational layer and

32

data abstract layer. A **view**, which is commonly referred as a template, is displayed to the user. These templates are completely separated from models and controllers.

There are two types of forms in Symfony framework.

- **Propel form** – Based on database table(s). These forms persist the submitted data to the table table(s) that they are based on.

- **Simple form** – This form generally follow the same approach as the Propel-based d forms.

All the configuration files of PHP Symfony framework are written in YAML format (http://www.yaml.org). At the first run Symfony reads the configuration and then written to cache as a native PHP array. Many of Symfony's features are customizable in the many configuration files. In Symfony, templates, partials, components, and actions can all be cached to speed up the response times. By default the cache is stored on the file system, but a small amend to one of the configuration files can easily swap this to another caching mechanism such as memcache, for example (Bowler. 2009).

The best features in Symfony are the plugins. The available plugins either help a developer in some way, or provide full, feature-rich applications. A few of the main plugins are:

- sfGuardPlugin: Web asset management

- sfSimpleBlog: SimpleBlog for your site

- sfSimpleCMSplugin: Create a CMS

- sfLucenePlugin: Integrates the Zend framework's search engine

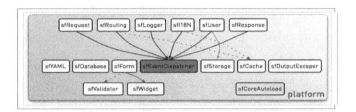

Figure 4.9: Symfony framework architecture

Source: http://www.symfony.com

To create a web application Symfony uses the Command Line Interface to make available tasks. These Symfony tasks do the following (Bowler. 2009):

- Generate the folder structure for a project, modules, applications and tasks

- Clear the generated cache and rotate log files

- Create controllers to enable and disable an application and set permissions.

- Interact with ORM layer to build models and forms

- Interact with SQL to insert data into the database

- Generate initial tests and execute them

Ruby on Rails (RoR)

Ruby on Rails as it is commonly referred to as, is a web framework built on the Ruby programming language. It integrates Model-View-Controller style connectivity between the data storage, business logic, and interface. In many other programming languages with their

34

frameworks such as Java, Perl and PHP, the developers had to understand about what does the specific lines of code do due to the framework is not designed to provide a common and linear view of the web application.

Ruby on Rails framework is supportable for Linux, Windows and MacOS X and it can be installed on various types of web servers such as LightSpeed, Lighttpd and Apache. Comparing with other more popular technologies like PHP, Perl etc, there are not many available hosts in the internet with Ruby on Rails supported. More known database drivers are exist for Ruby including DBMS, Oracle, MySQL and PostgreSQL. Beside from using web services to communicate with web applications developed using different technologies, not much libraries exist. Particular plugin called WebORB makes Ruby on Rails applications and Flash remote clients communicate each other (Bigg & Katz. 2011).

It is a key decision for all startups to choose a technology platform. The choice must be based on either technological or strategic point of view. To get more keener insight about Ruby on Rails analyze and study a little bit about its features in order to understand what really are the tradeoffs. Compared to some of the similar frameworks it appears that Ruby on Rails performing a little bit faster. It performs 30% faster comparing to Java Springs according to the test made by Gehtland(2009).

When implementing the same project, both Java using Spring framework and Ruby on Rails produced the following statistics in terms of implementing the same application.

	Lines of Code	Number of Classes	Number of Methods	Configuration Lines
Rails	1163	54	125	110
Java	3291	61	544	1154

Table 4.1: Lines of codes comparing Rails and Java

Source: http://www.serverside.com

The architecture of Ruby on Rails is at the core of 3 main concepts which are Mode, View and Controller (or shortly MVC). The reasons of the creation of MVC are the following:

- It isolates the business logic layer from the presentation layer

- It makes it clear where different types of code belong for easy maintenance.

Several studies have identified various crucial benefits of using the modern technologies to build up the web applications. It is obvious that the usage of the latest technologies are aiming to perform build-up process in relatively short periods of time than the previous web technologies do (such as PHP, ASP) which we used to familiar with. For instance, Ruby on Rails, an open source web development framework; in his book Hartl (2010) stated that since its debut in 2004, Ruby on Rails has rapidly become one of the most powerful and popular frameworks for building dynamic web applications. What makes Rails so beneficial is it uses the conception called Convention over Configuration which makes developers follow conventions while they're coding, leaving them with little configuration to do. For example, if you create a model class named "Account" the corresponding database table will be called "Accounts" and the controller class will be "AccountsController". With these kind of advanced techniques, Rails has benefited from a palpable sense of excitement, starting with the famous 15-minutes weblog video by Rails creator David Hansson, now updated as the 15-minute weblog using Rails 2 by Ryan Bates. These videos are a great way to show the power of Rails.

Hartl (2010) also stated that many old PHP and ASP web applications have the code allocated throughout the HTML. It makes very hard for not only the developers implementing the code but those designers who are trying to find the markups. In contrast to that, Ruby on Rails uses the MVC (Model-View-Controller) compound design pattern to solve this problem. It separates the business logic into "Model" layer, "View" layer and "Controller" layer. The

"Controller" layer interacts with Model and passes the required data to View. With these features the codes are easily shaped into structured, clean and flexible form.

4.4. Study Web Application Development Process

This sub-chapter discusses the processes of web application developing Symfony. The previous sub-chapter discussed about the core features and components of PHP Symfony framework. In order to develop a web application in exactly planned way, the following necessary steps have to be taken:

1. Create the skeleton folder structure – Symfony framework has many ways in which it can help the developer create applications with less efforts.

2. Build the database schema

3. Configuring the ORM layer

4. Generate the models, forms and filters

To demonstrate the process of development process, *milkshake shop* has taken as an example application. **Create the skeleton folder structure** – The process begins with in order to initiate the first fundamental elements of the application. A project will reside in milkshake directory. Therefore (Bowler. 2009):

```
$mkdir ~/workspace/milkshake && cd ~/workspace/milkshake
```

The next step is to generate the project file structure

```
$/home/badral/workspace/milkshake>symfony generate:project
~orm=Propel milkshake
```

Build the database schema – MySQL is the default database in Symfony. The most common way to generate the database is to write CREATE statement in SQL. But in Symfony database schema will be either YAML (default configuration which generates a schema.yml file in config folder) or XML file. When Symfont generates database models, they will be placed inside the /lib/model file.

Configure the ORM layer – The first file that Symfony reads is the ProjectConfiguration.class.php file. It allows developers to enable the Propel layer plugin for the application. The file located in /config folder.

Generate the models, forms and filters – When the task to generate models, forms and filters are is executed, the schema.xml file is parsed and then the ORM layer is generated based on it. At the terminal, following three tasks are executed:

```
$/home/badral/workspace/milkshake>symfony propel:build-model
```

```
$/home/badral/workspace/milkshake>symfony propel:build-forms
```

```
$/home/badral/workspace/milkshake>symfony propel:build-filters
```

These tasks generate the entire ORM layer and all generated classes are located in a /lib folder (Bowler. 2009).

4.5. Features of the Technology for Web Applications

All known web application technologies assimilate and differ from each other with the certain features provided depending on purpose to increase the productivity. This sub-chapter covers the features of the latest emerging framework Ruby on Rails. To mention some of the main features of Ruby on Rails (RoR) framework:

- **MVC architecture**: RoR is based on the MVC (Model View Controller) architecture which separates data and presentation.

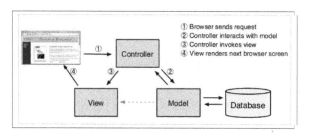

Figure 4.8: MVC Diagram

Source: (Smith & Nichols. 2007, p.93)

- **Database Access Library**: RoR includes a database access library - Active Record - Simplifies data handling in databases. Active Record automatically maps tables to classes and rows to objects.

- **Libraries for common tasks**: Ruby on Rails includes a host of libraries that simplify the coding of common programming tasks such as form validations, sessions management, etc.

- **AJAX Library**: An extensive library of AJAX functions is provided in the Rails framework. Ruby code can be used to generate AJAX code. The associated java scripting required for AJX gets generated automatically.

- **Convention over configuration**: RoR does not use any XML configuration files. Instead it includes programming conventions that can be used to specify the configuration parameters.

- **Customized URL**: Custom or Search Engine Friendly URLs can be developed using the Ruby on Rails framework.

39

- **Debugging**: Detailed error logs are provided, making it easier to debug applications.

- **Components**: Components can be used to store reusable code. Components can be included to modularize templates.

- **Object-Relational Mapping:** ORM libraries map tables database table to classes. If a database has a table called *orders*, our program will have a class named *Order*. Rows in this table correspond to objects of the class—a particular order is represented as an object of class *Order*. Within that object, attributes are used to get and set the individual columns.

And the MVCs are explained in detailed:

- **M**odels – This layer mostly deals with an application' data. Models are primarily used for managing the rules of interaction with a corresponding database tables. And in most cases, every table in the database interacts to one model in the web application. The table of database is named after the plural object: posts, books, students. Model file has the following features:

  - Contain data manipulation methods

  - Contain validation rules

  - Is named after the singular object (for instance: post.rb, book.rb, student.rb)

- **V**iew – The view represents the data to the user. Every action within a controller could have a view file which is RHTML file type named after corresponding action. This RHTML file is HTML file with the Ruby codes inside. The whole application could have a default layer (for instance, application.rhtml) and each controller may have its own layout named after representing plural object (for instance, posts.rhtml, books.rhtml).

- Controller – The controller could be considered as the internal engine of the application. It receives data and events from the user, triggers the model to process required application data, and generates the view to present the resulting data to the user. Every object in the Rails application also has its own controller file as it has its own view file:

    o Contains methods and events

    o Contains actions with mostly 3 to 5 lines of codes

    o No SQL

    o Named after plural object (for instance books.rb, posts.rb).

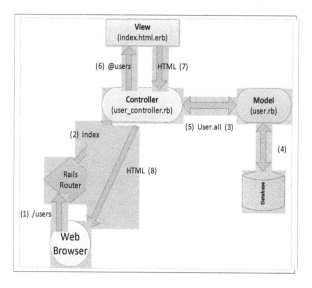

Figure 4.9: A detailed diagram of MVC Rails

41

Source: (Hartl. 2008)

An underlying principle of Ruby on Rails is that of **convention over configuration**. Basically, this means that the designers of the framework have broken the workings of a web application into its core components. Conventions have allowed the core components to be standardized, and thereby access to them is greatly simplified.

In Smith & Nichols (2007) noted that this convention features allowed the core components to be standardized, and thereby access to them is greatly simplified. For example, there is a list called *bags*. Rails convention is to save the list in database table called *bags*. The convention then prescribes that each line of data can be represented by an object that is the singular of the table name. So if our table is bags, the object that can hold data from the tables is a *Bag* object. Fields in the table are automatically converted to properties of the object. So if there is a *color* field, the object will have this property; that is, *bag.color*. All you need is to create the database schema, define the database connection in a single configuration file, and your application will be able to create your bags table and use the data in the table as Bag objects. And saving a new bag to the database will be simple as:

```
next_bag = Bag.new
next_bag.color = "Black"
next_bag.save
```

In three lines *Bag* object was created, defined the color as black, and saved it to the database. Thanks to the Rails conventions, the system knows automatically to save the data into a table called bags, and to enter the text Black into the *color* field.

4.6.   Web Applications by Chosen Technology

Ruby on Rails users run the gamut from scrappy startups to huge companies like: Twitter, Posterous, 37signals, Scribd, Hulu and the Yellow Pages – the list of the sites using Rails goes on and on.

Figure 4.10: Few of the known applications built on Ruby on Rails

Source: http://www.rubyonrails.org

Also it can be distinguishable the websites on the internet using Ruby on Rails by the category. The following chart diagram represents the industry distribution of the top 100,000 websites currently active by Ruby on Rails:

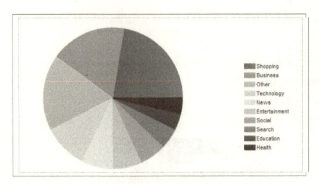

Figure 4.11: Distribution of Ruby on Rails usage

Source: http://serverside.com

From the diagram above it is clear that Ruby on Rails is most likely to be found in use on Shopping, Business or Technology websites. Within this result more than 14,000 websites are the most visited sites on the Internet and an additional over 200,000 websites on the rest of the web.

4.7. Web Applications by Other Popular Platforms

In this sub-chapter some wide-spread web applications which built with common types of programming languages (e.g. PHP, ASP.NET, Python, Java, CGI) are covered in briefly.

The following list shows the most influential web applications made by PHP language ():

- phpMyAdmin – A tool written in PHP designed to handle the administration of MySQL over the web. It performs create and drop databases. Development was made by phpMyAdmin team.

- SquirrelMail – SquirrelMail is web-based mailing package. It supports IMAP and SMTP protocols. It has all the features and functionalities that email user could demand, including MIME (Multipurpose Internet Mail Extensions)..

- Drupal – Drupal is one of the most popular modular content management system, blogging, forum and community engines. It has the features include discussion, forums, content rating, content versioning, taxonomy support and it also can be used as web application framework (http://www.blog.fedecarg.com).

5. Design and Implementation

This thesis widely covers about e-commerce systems and its property, behaviors to set a demonstration of the usage of the modern web technology in this type of systems.

Like architecture of any other web applications e-commerce systems maintain electronic payment and online transactions. Components of the e-commerce systems have connected each other under continuous procedure which buy and sale.

In this chapter the demonstration application will be designed and implemented to show off some comparisons between particular similar applications. The resulting application will allow us to interact with it through its URLs, giving us insight into the benefits and advantage features of Ruby on Rails application. As with forthcoming sample application, the web application will consist of users and their associated e-commerce modules (thus constituting a minimalist web design application).

5.1. Collecting Information

Software development projects require desired information to build the system. Gathering the appropriate data onwards the designing and implementing the real development is the crucial point for successful project. This diploma thesis mainly issues the demonstration of the specific module of medium sized e-commerce (electronic commerce) implemented by particular programming language. Collecting information may fit in the following sequence of steps:

1. Specify the possible requirement of the system

2. Determine the technology tools for development

3. Define the data tables for application database

46

5.2. Introduction of the System Purpose

There are dozens of e-commerce software which can be classified as commercial and free open-source. The biggest software applications are Volusion, Shopify, Ashop Commerce (Microsoft) etc. Beside these familiar products there are open-source applications with free software license as well. The e-commerce software may include several components in order to combine one complete system. This thesis issues the general components to demonstrate the utilization of modern web developing technology.

The web applications are all have their specific internal structures and consistent architecture depending on the business goal which it is being developed to aim and the technology in which is being used to maintain it. As described in the previous chapters the basis application is e-commerce system. Thereby e-commerce system itself has its own structure which comprised the definite modules. The typical structure in e-commerce systems is as following:

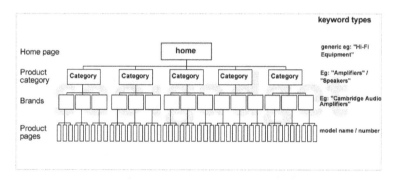

Figure 5.1: Structure of e-commerce system

Source: http://seogadget.co.uk

The demonstration module consists of the following modules. In Ruby on Rails framework each of the modules represent as the complex objects connected with each other by containing

47

database table structure (Model), HTML web page (View) and manipulation file (Controller) reconciling the Model with View. General modules in e-commerce application are:

- Administration (Administration module where modify the settings of the web site including add, update, delete products)

- Account (Contains the account information of the user including, credit card information, history of the order etc.)

- Users (Customers who want to make a trade)

- User Sessions (Handling the session of the active user in the website)

- Products (Products)

- Property (Property of the product, e.g. size, color)

- Shipping zone (Specific zone areas in which the order can be shipped)

- Shipping methods (Different ways of shipping the order, e.g. UPS Ground, 2 Day Air)

- Cart (Stores the products which the user is about to make a trade with)

- Shipping Category (Where the category of the shipping is classified by representing shipping methods and shipping rates)

- Brands (Identifies the brand of the product. Many products could belong to a single brand)

- Prototype (A part of the product which identifies the product itself)

5.3.   Specifying the System Architecture

General perspective of the system is described as Class diagram:

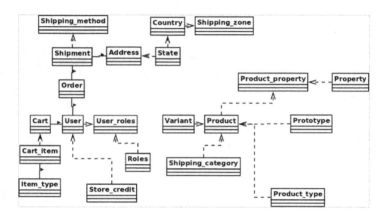

Figure 5.2: Class diagram of the application

5.4.   Establishing the Design Features

The typical first step when making a web application is to create a data model, which is the representation of the structures needed by our application. In our case, the web application will be concentrated on stripping-down module functionalities with users. Thus, it begins with a model for *users* of the application and then with a model for *modules*.

There are as many choices for a user data model as there are different registration forms on the web; it will go with a distinctly minimalist approach. Users of our web application will have a unique integer identifier called id (or User ID), a publicly viewer name (of type string), a password (of type string), Encrypted password (Password in encrypted form), Account ID (Indicates the account of the user), Language (language used by user), and 'Created at' that

49

shows the creation date of the user by administrator. A summary of the data model for users appears in the following:

User	
id	integer
First name	string
Last name	string
Birth date	date
email	string
state	string
Account id	integer
Password salt	string
Encrypted password	String
Comments count	integer
Created at	datetime
Updated at	datetime

Table 5.1: User data table

The User instance belongs to account and has many orders, phones, addresses, roles, wish lists, shipping addresses and shopping carts

As for the models of e-commerce modules, let's take an instance of Product module. The module has one table which contains one record for every fixed asset:

Product	
id	integer
name	string
description	string
Product keywords	string
Product type id	integer
Prototype id	integer
Shipping category id	integer
Permalink	string
Available at	datetime
Deleted at	datetime
Meta keywords	string
Meta description	string
Created at	datetime
Updated at	datetime
active	boolean
Brand id	integer

Table 5.2: Product data model

Since the Product model is represented by consolidating the other features; each product belongs to Brand, Product type, Prototype and Shipping category. Also Product has dependent on various features; therefore has many product properties, variants and images.

Implementing data model along with web interface to that model is simply easy in Rails. The *Users* data model has a combination constitutes *Users resource,* which will allow it to think of users as objects that can be created, read, updated, and deleted through the web via the HTTP protocol. The Users resource will be created by a scaffold generator program, which comes standard with each Rails project. The argument of the scaffold commands is the singular version of the resource name (in this case, User) together with optional parameters for the data models attributes:

```
$ RAILS GENERATE SCAFFOLD ID: INTEGER FIRST_NAME: STRING LAST_NAME:
STRING BIRTH_DATE: DATE EMAIL: STRING STATE: STRING
ACCOUNT_ID: INTEGER PASSWORD_SALT: STRING ENCRYPTED_PASSWORD:
STRING COMMENTS_COUNT: INTEGER CREATED_AT: DATETIME
UPDATED_AT: DATETIME

INVOKE ACTIVE_RECORD

CREATE DB/MIGRATE/20111213004000_CREATE_USERS.RB

CREATE APP/MODELS/USER.RB

INVOKE TEST_UNIT

CREATE TEST/UNIT/USER_TEST.RB

CREATE TEST/FIXTURES/USERS.YML

ROUTE RESOURCES :USERS

INVOKE SCAFFOLD_CONTROLLER

CREATE APP/CONTROLLERS/USERS_CONTROLLER.RB

INVOKE ERB

CREATE APP/VIEWS/USERS

CREATE APP/VIEWS/USERS/INDEX.HTML.ERB

CREATE APP/VIEWS/USERS/EDIT.HTML.ERB

CREATE APP/VIEWS/USERS/SHOW.HTML.ERB

CREATE APP/VIEWS/USERS/NEW.HTML.ERB

CREATE APP/VIEWS/USERS/_FORM.HTML.ERB

INVOKE TEST_UNIT

CREATE TEST/FUNCTIONAL/USERS_CONTROLLER_TEST.RB

INVOKE HELPER

CREATE APP/HELPERS/USERS_HELPER.RB

INVOKE STYLESHEETS
```

52

```
CREATE PUBLIC/STYLESHEETS/SCAFFOLD.CSS
```

By including **id:integer** and **first_name: string** etc. it has arranged for the User model to have the form shown in Table 5.2. To proceed with the application, it's needed to `migrate` the database using *Rake* command. Rake command is the compilation of the database in Rails framework:

```
$ RAKE DB:MIGRATE

==    CREATEUSERS:  MIGRATING
========================================

--    CREATE_TABLE ( : USERS)

      -> 0.0017s

==  CREATEUSERS:  MIGRATED  (0.0018s)
==============================
```

This simply updates the database with our new **Users** data model.

An user has an account. And in the account there are identifications which represents Addresses, Credit Cards, Orders and User Profiles

Figure 5.4 Account view of the User

Some specific design model has been carried out in Shopping cart module. As indicated above each User has many Carts and Cart items. Therefore the data model must be look like as shown below:

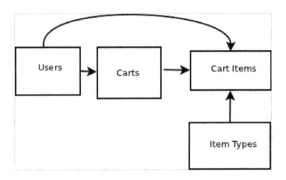

Figure 5.5: Shopping cart data model

Here Item type represents the state of the item and allows you to view all the items the user ever put in their cart. Item types are:

- Shopping cart

- Wish list

- Purchased

A Variant is a specific type of product. If a product is red (e.g. Blue or Green) Large then it could have these 4 variants:

- Small Red

- Large Red

- Small Green

- Large Green

Checkout process by user is classified into 2 types: Pre-Checkout and Checkout.

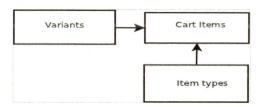

Figure 5.6: Pre-checkout model

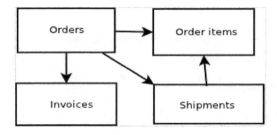

Figure 5.7: Checkout model

When the user clicks checkout the order is created from the shopping cart. And user cannot go to the final checkout screen until they confirmed:

- Login

- Add a shipping address

- Add a shipping method

- Order items are associated to the order

Once the checkout has completed the invoice is created.

An order can have many shipments. Thus a shipment does not need to have all the order items and it has many order items instead of just belonging to the order. It is charged at Shipment.

6. Comparison to Other Similar System

In this chapter analytical part of the developed and other similar applications will be explained. The main features of the particular frameworks which highlighted during the development process of the applications will be described in detail. For example, Validation handing during the user login or sign up process.

6.1. Analysis of the Developed System

Analytical approach is mainly based on the particular terms in Ruby on Rails features which are following:

- ⋏ HTTP responses in coding level

- ⋏ Maintenance of the database designing in coding level

- ⋏ Convention over configuration

Session manipulation

Ruby on Rails provides two modes to store sessions. In the database-store mode, the session is stored in the database with identifier of keyed value. Another mode is cookie-stored mode which stores the session in the cookie.

```
14      session[:authenticated_at] = Time.now
15      cookies[:insecure] = false
16      ## if there is a cart make sure the user_id is correct
```

Figure 6.1: Set current time value to logged in user's session

(user_sessions_controller.rb file)

In this picture system current time is set to the value of the user's session. The field **:authenticated_at** identifies the time when user logged into the system. But unfortunately, in this case the code is vulnerable: if some user fails to log into the system, then the user can reply the session.

Creating responses

HTTP response functionality can be seen from the controller's point of view. Generally there are 3 types of HTTP response in Rails framework.

- ⋏ `render`: A full response to the browser

- ⋏ `redirect_to`: HTTP status code to the browser

- ⋏ `head`: Consistent of HTTP header to the browser

In the e-commerce application the first two methods of sending HTTP response is widely used.

```
1 <%= render :partial => '/admin/config/sub_header'%>
2
3 <h1> Shipping Zones</h1>
```

Figure 6.2: Render partial attribute
(admin/config/shipping_zones/index.html.erb)

A *partial* is combination of HTML and Ruby code and it can be reused in multiple places. This would render "/admin/config/_sub_header.html.erb" and pass the instance variable @sub_header in as a local variable to the template for display. In other words it actually

58

attaches the contents in */_sub_header.html.erb* to the file
/admin/config/shipping_zones/index.html.erb.

Another way to manage the return processes to an HTTP request is `redirect_to`. This
method tells the browser to send a new request for another different URL.

```
10        if current_user && current_user.admin?
11           redirect_to admin_merchandise_products_url
12        else
13           redirect_to login_url
14        end
15      end
```

Figure 6.3: Redirect method usage (`welcome_controller.rb`)

In the line 10, it checks whether a user is logged in and user is *admin* then the browser makes
a request for `admin_merchandise_products` page. Otherwise it redirects to *login*
page.

Another special usage of `redirect_to` is send the user back to the page just came from:

```
19    if current_user && current_user.admin?
20       flash[:alert] = 'Sorry you are not allowed to do that.'
21       redirect_to :back
22    else
```

Figure 6.4: Redirect method usage with the field value

The usage of **:back** field is identical to *Back* button in the browser which goes back to the
previous visited page.

In Ruby on Rails connection between the application and database is handled through the
query interface **ActiveRecord.**

First, to create the database tables in Ruby code it needs to generate *model* by given
command. For example, as for *Products* model:

59

```
rails generate model product
        Model: app/model/product.rb
        Test:  test/unit/product_test.rb
        Fixtures: test/fixtures/products.yml
        Migration: db/migrate/001_create_product.rb
```

Here, in the directory db/migrate the file *001_create_product.rb* is generated automatically in which the database table fields are gonna be created.

```
 1 class CreateProducts < ActiveRecord::Migration
 2   def self.up
 3     create_table :products do |t|
 4       t.string        :name,               :null => false
 5       t.text          :description
 6       t.text          :product_keywords
 7       t.integer       :tax_category_id
 8       t.integer       :product_type_id,    :null => false
 9       t.integer       :prototype_id
10       t.integer       :shipping_category_id,  :null => false
11       t.integer       :tax_status_id,      :null => false
12       t.string        :permalink,          :null => false
13       t.datetime      :available_at
14       t.datetime      :deleted_at
15       t.string        :meta_keywords
16       t.string        :meta_description
17       t.boolean       :featured,           :default => false
18       #t.integer       :count_on_hand
19       t.timestamps
```

Figure 6.5: Product table in *001_create_product.rb* file

Class name *CreateProducts* is automatically inherited from ActiveRecord query interface. In order to update the database with a new data model (e.g. MySQL, sqlite3 or PostgreSQL); the command `rake db:migrate` is run from the command-line. If there is some mistake occurred by the developer and it needs to be changed, then first `rake db:rollback` command must be executed in order to roll back the mistaken changes and re-run the command `rake db:migrate` to apply the new changes.

Designing database tables in the level of the diagram (for example, using class diagrams for specifying the fields and attributes) are popular method by putting and linking the tables with the lines and specifying the corresponding fields and functionalities. Ruby on Rails provides some designing of database tables during the runtime. It goes with the attributes like `has_many`, `has_one` and `has_and_belongs_to_many` expressing how many related objects belong to the particular object and contrary, where does that particular object belong to.

For example, after generating model for a object `Shipping_category`, Ruby automatically created a file `shipping_category.rb` in **/app/models** directory.

```
1  class ShippingCategory < ActiveRecord::Base
2    #belongs_to :product
3    has_many :products
4    has_many :shipping_rates
5
6    validates :name,            :presence => true,        :length =>
     { :maximum => 255 }
7  end
```

Figure 6.6: Shipping category dependency with other objects

61

In above figure, it shows that the Shipping_category may contain many *Products* and Shipping_rates. In the contrary, Shipping_rates belongs to a single

```
17 class ShippingRate < ActiveRecord::Base
18   include ActionView::Helpers::NumberHelper
19
20   belongs_to :shipping_method
21   belongs_to :shipping_rate_type
22
23   belongs_to  :shipping_category
24   has_many    :products
25
26   validates  :rate,                    :presence =>
   true, :numericality => true
27
28   validates  :shipping_method_id,      :presence => true
29   validates  :shipping_rate_type_id,   :presence => true
30   validates  :shipping_category_id,    :presence => true
```

Shipping_category and other objects. Another term of linkage as for Shipping_rates object is:

Figure 6.7: Shipping_rates belongs to several objects at a time

From the figure we see shipping_rates belongs to several objects which have identical properties. At the same time the it ensures that the objects it linked to should have values to be presented in the database table. It indicates that those objects are required to have a valid data to be stored in the database.

The term convention over configuration is the one of the main features of Ruby on Rails framework. It means that by default any model name is mapped to a table with the same name. It allows the developers to choose the name of the model and database table they want.

Every Rails application contains the configuration files with YML and RB extensions. The core configuration files which define the application and database settings are *application.rb*, *database.yml* and *routes.rb*.

```
 3 development:
 4   adapter: sqlite3
 5   database: db/development.sqlite3
 6   username: root
 7   pool: 5
 8   timeout: 5000
 9
10 ## Warning: The database defined as "test" will |
11 ## re-generated from your development database w|
```

Figure 6.8: database.yml configuration file of e-commerce application

Sqlite3 database engine is the default engine for Rails applications. Other database engines are MySQL and PostgreSQL allowed to work with Rails application and configuration can be in the file at the directory /app/config/database.yml.

```
 2
 3   resources :user_sessions, :only => [:new, :create, :destroy]
 4
 5   match 'admin'    => 'admin/overviews#index'
 6   match 'login'    => 'user_sessions#new'
 7   match 'logout'   => 'user_sessions#destroy'
 8   match 'signup'   => 'customer/registrations#new'
 9   match 'admin/merchandise' => 'admin/merchandise/summary#index'
```

Figure 6.9: routes.rb configuration file

In the above figure parameter `resources :user_sessions` creates seven different routes in the application.

HTTP Verb	Path	Action	Used for
GET	/user_sessions	index	Display a list of all user sessions
GET	/user_sessions	new	Return an HTML form for creating a new user session
POST	/user_sessions	create	Create a new user session
GET	/user_sessions/:id	show	Display a specific user session
GET	/user_sessions:id/edit	edit	Return an HTML form for editing user session
PUT	/user_sessions/:id	update	Update a specific user session
DELETE	/user_sessions/:id	destroy	Delete a specific user session

Table 6.1: Routes for user_session

Since the session of user does not need to be edited or showed on the web page, therefore it routes only *new*, *create* or *destroy* are allowed. The match attribute asks the router to match the receiving GET request to a controller action. In the Figure 6.9, **match** "admin" indicates that */admin* permalink always show the home page (or *index.html.erb*) of the */admin_overview* controller.

6.2.   Analysis of the Other Developed System

The e-commerce is very widespread term which has been implemented variety of people and organizations. There are dozens of free and commercial shopping cart systems are being used present day. In this sub-chapter **Opencart** shopping cart system was chosen to compare to the currently developed e-commerce web application. Opencart system is PHP-based free e-commerce application with the variety of features provided.

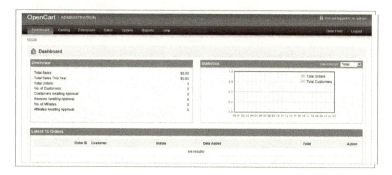

Figure 6.10: Administration dashboard of Opencart

Similar to the most of the modern web applications Opencart uses MVC (Model-View-Controller) architecture.

Opencart database creation has the same process as the process of other PHP-based web applications and is fully dependable from the Apache PhpMyAdmin working with 92 tables in total. During the installation database name should be created in PhpMyAdmin.

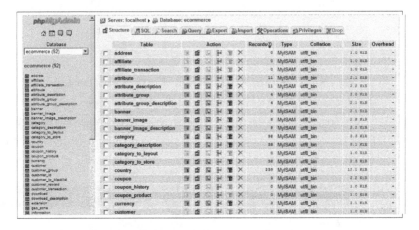

Figure 6.11: Opencart database tables

Opencart application has built in using MVC architecture. The application has main modules which are **Admin** and **Catalog.** Each of the modules contains MVC modules which also contains sub-modules. As for View, both of the modules share one common web interface designing (including, images, styleshee css, themes) applied for all their sub-modules.

The sub-modules in Admin module are controllable only by the Administrator. For example, the administrator has a full permission to add, update or delete the catalog or corresponding product which is contained as a sub-module in Admin module.

The sub-modules which have Controller within the Admin module:

- ⅄ catalog – Includes Products, Manufacturers, Product category informations can be modified by the administrator

- ⅄ design – Banner and layout of the admin module

- ⅄ localization – includes country, geo zone, language, stock and tax status

- ⅄ sale – includes information for coupon, order, voucher and contact

66

- setting – Manipulates the global settings (language, currency and validation of the information entries in the text field)

- user – Controls the users and user permissions

- payment – Controls item payment and checkout process

- report – Shows the history information for sales (shipping, sale coupon, sale tax, and sale return etc.)

- shipping – controls the shipping process (item weight, delivery object)

- feed – Controls feeding of the web page

- error – Shows the possible invalid access warning pages of the application (not found pages, permission of the pages)

- total – Shows the total informations for the coupon, credit, voucher, tax, order and rewards of the user

These sub-modules in the controller has the common 4 functionalities. For example, User controller in Admin module performs the following main functionalities:

HTTP verb	Action	Used for
GET	index	Shows the list of the object
POST	Insert	Adds a new user to the database table
POST	Update	Edits the current user information in the table
DELETE	Delete	Deletes the current user from the table

Table 6.2: Functionalities of the sub-modules in Admin module

```
15      public function insert() {
16      $this->load->language('user/user');
17
18      $this->document->setTitle($this->language->get('heading_title'));
19
20          $this->load->model('user/user');
21
22      if (($this->request->server['REQUEST_METHOD'] == 'POST') && $this->validateForm()) {
23              $this->model_user_user->addUser($this->request->post);
24
25          $this->session->data['success'] = $this->language->get('text_success');
26
27          $url = '';
28
29          if (isset($this->request->get['sort'])) {
30              $url .= '&sort=' . $this->request->get['sort'];
31          }
32
```

Figure 6.12: Insertion of a new user by administrator

In the above figure, it calls the `addUser($this->request->post)` function (at the line 23) to add a new user to the table. If we look at the `User.php` file in the directory **/admin/model/**:

```
1 <?php
2 class ModelUserUser extends Model {
3       public function addUser($data) {
4           $this->db->query("INSERT INTO '" . DB_PREFIX . "user' SET username = '" . $this->db->escape($data
['username']) . "', password = '" . $this->db->escape(md5($data['password'])) . "', firstname = '" . $this->db->escape($data
['firstname']) . "', lastname = '" . $this->db->escape($data['lastname']) . "', email = '" . $this->db->escape($data
['email']) . "', user_group_id = '" . (int)$data['user_group_id'] . "', status = '" . (int)$data['status'] . "', date_added
= NOW()");
5       }
```

Figure 6.13: Adding a new user to the table

The function AddUser executes the simple query statement (SQL commands) in order to insert the user information into the database table. The **app/model** directory has the corresponding files for each sub-modules in Admin module. These model files contain the functions executing the query statements (for example, addUser, editUser and editPassword and deleteUser).

The configuration files in Opencart are categorized into 2 parts. One is for Admin module and another is for Catalog module configuration. These configuration files allow to use the global constant variables which could be attached in the module Admin, Catalog respectively. Besides these configuration files it has one global configuration file called php.ini which encircles the entire application.

```
 1 magic_quotes_gpc = Off;
 2 register_globals = Off;
 3 default_charset = UTF-8;
 4 memory_limit = 64M;
 5 max_execution_time = 18000;
 6 upload_max_filesize = 999M;
 7 safe_mode = Off;
 8 mysql.connect_timeout = 20;
 9 session.use_cookies = On;
10 session.use_trans_sid = Off;
11 session.gc_maxlifetime = 12000000;
12 allow_url_fopen = on;
13 ;display_errors = 1;
14 ;error_reporting = E_ALL;
```

Figure 6.13: Configuration file php.ini

The file indicates the global settings for the application setting providing various types of values for whether it is allowed to use cookies in session or to define the memory size of the application.

Ordering process in Opencart system is very sophisticated issue. The lines of codes which proceed the confirmation of the order checkout take around 400. If we take a look at the file `confirm.php` file in the directory `catalogy/controller/checkout`, which makes the final confirmation process of the customer order; the defined steps are the following:

1. First it checks the validation whether shipping address has been set

2. Checks the validation if the shipping method has been set

3. Validates if the address of payment has been set

4. Validates if the method of payment has been set

5. Checks whether cart has the product and stock

6. Checks the minimum quantity of the products ordered

7. Sets all the information of the customer, payment shipping to the `data` package which will be sent as the argument between the two pages.

8. Sets the gift voucher of the product to the `data` package.

9. Sets all the product information to the `data` package.

```
118            if ($this->customer->isLogged()) {
119                $data['customer_id'] = $this->customer->getId();
120                $data['customer_group_id'] = $this->customer->getCustomerGroupId();
121                $data['firstname'] = $this->customer->getFirstName();
122                $data['lastname'] = $this->customer->getLastName();
123                $data['email'] = $this->customer->getEmail();
124                $data['telephone'] = $this->customer->getTelephone();
125                $data['fax'] = $this->customer->getFax();
126
127            $this->load->model('account/address');
```

Figure 6.14: Sample lines of coding of the checkout confirmation

In the above figure, it shows that data package argument which holds the all information relevant to order checkout process and is being sent to the next page as an argument of the function.

6.3.   Comparing the Systems On Behalf Of the Technology

As we seen in the previous chapter, analyses for both different frameworks show the different perspectives in some ways. First and foremost is the complementary software to form the development environment. To do web application and to run the completed one under Ruby on Rails framework needed no external software such as what we use for PHP framework. Because we have to install the several external programs such as local web server (e.g. XAMP or WAMP) in order to execute PHP application. But in the case of Ruby on Rails no external web server needed install in the local computer. All we need is install the packages in order where Ruby language goes first and then Gem (which handles packages and is a standard library of Ruby installation since Ruby version 1.9), finally Rails which deploys a installable package of the framework.

The next important thing is, the number of lines of codes is considered as extremely dissimilar issues as for the developers. When a developer works on the application building with Ruby on Rails framework it takes from a developer far less dealing than it would take working on PHP based framework. For example, User controller has the same actions which are index, create (insert in PHP), update, delete for both frameworks.

e-commerce built in Ruby on Rails	Opencart system built in PHP
87	500
(app/controller/admin/users_controller.rb)	(admin/controller/users/users.php)

Table 6.3: Lines of codes in both User controllers

Not only in controllers but also it differentiates in views and model files. Especially model files in Opencart contain huge number of SQL commands that take hundreds of lines. In contrast Ruby on Rails model files have relatively less lines of codes due to the fact it does not use SQL.

e-commerce built in Ruby on Rails	Opencart system built in PHP
Direct mapping to the tables	PhpMyAdmin tool
Sqlite3 (Default), MySQL, PostgreSQL	MicrosoftSQL, MySQL, PostgreSQL, Sqlite

Table 6.4: Database usage for both systems

Database migration process in Ruby on Rails is relatively flexible where developer can easily modify database tables even during the run time. Dependency between the tables also identified in the files in **app/models** directory when it uses the attributes such as has_one, has_many, belongs_to etc. Opencart system is fully dependent on PhpMyAdmin tool which handles the administration of MySQL. In contrary Ruby on Rails database designing is independent of SQL in the level of coding where a model in Ruby on Rails framework maps directly to a table in a database. And developers are allowed to choose whatever model name

72

and table name. In the case of when a developer mistakenly has some errors on **app/model** designing he is able to re-migrate the database by rolling back the tables and migrating again. This feature gives more privileges to a Ruby on Rails developer to make changes simultaneously rather than making the changes in separate tool which is totally independent from the ongoing web application.

And the next thing is the gap of the configuration files in both systems in terms of number. Opencart system has plenty numbers of configuration files when two main categories Admin and Catalog have the separate setting files where the files are almost identical. Ruby on Rails has the some main configuration files with YML extension which fully spans the entire application. For example `database.yml` and `config.yml` files can be the total solutions configuring the entire in our e-commerce application where Opencart still has the different types of configuration files in dispersed into its main modules of Admin and Catalog.

7. Experimental Results and Analysis

In this part it will briefly summarize the experiences which obtained during the development of the web applications and consequences comparing the features in two separate platforms.

7.1. Gained Experiences

The e-commerce web application is fully functional application which provides the people sell and trade the goods through online. By doing this thesis it has obtained some acknowledged know-hows and knowledge on putting e-commerce on the web programming paradigm. Varieties of web development technology have been established since the last few decades. From those technologies it has chosen Ruby on Rails to challenge my development and being able to bring my skill to a new level. Developing Ruby on Rails allows developer to work in flexible environment using all-in-one methods. Data collection was the crucial stage in the beginning of this thesis. Finding a proper data and variables for the web application is important to keep the development up on the right side. It took much more time for gathering the information and building the design of database tables rather than implementation of coding. Also it required to find the proper open-source platform which built in either PHP based framework or Python based one.

After successfully assembled the data which is needed for the application it is required to create the development environment. Creating the environment under Ruby on Rails framework is considered as a deal to accomplish in shortly which is an extended advantage for Ruby developers. Because no third party software required (such as local web servers

As for the implementation part of the application the initial thing was how to create the database tables dynamically on the basis of linkages between the tables that already done in the design part.

74

8. Conclusion and Future Work

In this thesis it has analyzed the usability of Ruby on Rails framework and made the comparison of it based on the e-commerce web application with another identical application built in PHP framework. Comparing to PHP based framework the result showed that the Rails developers obtain more productivity by writing less code and getting a light environmental settings of the development. A developer of Ruby on Rails can be apart from writing the complicated configuration files and is allowed to smoothly handle the database table designing during the runtime. In addition, a database migration process of Ruby on Rails showed that a developer can spare the time when creating the database schema and switching between the versions of database.

During the study and analyzes it has tried to put my effort to emphasize the features and advantage of Ruby on Rails framework over those typical features of PHP base frameworks. Electronic shopping applications based on PHP technology has been popularized among the web developers through the years. Almost many of their database based on PhpMyAdmin tools with consolidation of local web servers such as XAMP or WAMP. Opencart system is free, reliable to use and considered as one of those shopping systems despite its open-source designation. The system has built in using the logic of MVC architecture which indicates objects in class has its controller, view and model elements. It also provides very sophisticated procedures of electronic shopping system controlling over 90 tables in database. Considering analysis made in this thesis it has come to the conclusion that the web applications with PHP framework including Opencart is less handy and comfortable for the developers comparing with e-commerce application built in Ruby on Rails. In addition Ruby language's dynamic, reflective and composition of the different syntaxes make Ruby on Rails framework much handy in terms of usability and offer a temper proceeding for both the coding and designing database table at the same time.

Future analysis and investigations need to be done to evaluate Ruby on Rails deployment performance and scalability. Also the debugging technique in Ruby on Rails provides very detailed log information to the developer which needed to be considered to run the development with prudent approaches.

9. Bibliography

[1]   Hartl, M. Ruby on Rails 3 Tutorial: Learn Rails by Example. Addison Wesley, 2010. 544p. ISBN-13: 978-0-321-74312-1

[2]   Shklar, L., and Rozen, R. Web application architecture: Principles, protocols and practices. John Wiley and Sons Ltd, 2003. 374p. ISBN: 0-471-48656-6

[3]   Lane, D., and Williams, H.E. Web database Application with PHP and MySQL, 2nd edition. O'Reilly Media, 2004. 816p. ISBN: 0-596-00543-1

[4]   Deacon, J. Model-View-Controller (MVC) Architecture. Research paper. Revised May 2009. 6p. Official source: http://www.jdl.co.uk/briefings/index.html#mvc

[5]   Spaanjaars, I. Beginning ASP.NET 4 in C# and VB. Wiley Publishing, 2010. 777p. ISBN: 978-0-470-50221-1

[6]   Porebski, B., and Nowak, L. Building PHP Applications with Symfony, CakePHP, and Zend Framework. Wiley Publishing, 2011. 1235p. ISBN: 978-0-470-88734-9

[7]   Bowler, T., and Bancer, W. Symfony 1.3 Web Application Development. Packt Publishing, 2009. 211p. ISBN: 978-1-847194-56-5

[8]   Bigg, R., and Katz, W. Rails 3 in Action. Manning Publishing Co., 2011. 592p. ISBN: 978-1-935182-27-6

[9]   Gehtland, J. Spring: A Developer's Notebook, 1st edition. O'Reilly Media, 2009. 216p. ASIN: B00260R2HW

[10]   Smith, E., and Nichols, R. Ruby on Rails: Enterprise Application Development, Plan, Program, Extend. Packt Publishing, 2007. 525p. ISBN: 978-1-847190-85-7

[11]   Fitzgerald, E., and D.Guy. Information systems development: Methodologies, techniques and tools. 6th edition. McGraw Hill Higher Education, 2006. 656p. ISBN 0077114175

[12]   Tutorial website for Ruby on Rails platform: http://ruby.railstutorial.org/ [online].

[13]   Ruby on Rails: http://www.rubyonrails.com/ [online]

[14]   IBM – United States: http://www.ibm.com/ [online]

[15]   High Performance PHP Framework for Web Development: http://www.symfony.com/ [online]

[16]   Microsoft Licensing, Product Roadmaps: http://www.directionsmicrosoft.com/ [online]

[17]   Applets – Java: http://java.sun.com/ [online]

[18]   Simcrest – Microsoft Dynamics Nav: http://www.simcrest.com/ [online]

[19]   Learn Networking: http://www.learn-networking.com/ [online]

10.   Appendix

10.3.   Distribution of the Platforms in E-Commerce Websites

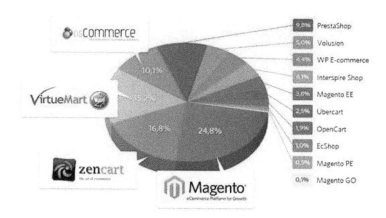

Source: http://www.simonlilly.com

10.4.   Usability of Various Web Application Platforms

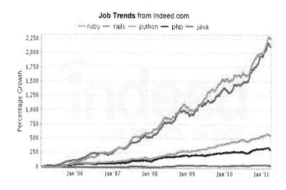

Source: http://articles.businessinsider.com

10.5.   Lines of Codes in MVC Including Comments

	e-commerce (Ruby on Rails)	Opencart system (Admin module)	Opencart system (Catalog module)
Controller	4078	36769	16883
Model	4867	7310	6102
View	6792	22438	7049
Total	15737	96551	

Source: own estimation

www.ingramcontent.com/pod-product-compliance
Lightning Source LLC
Chambersburg PA
CBHW051209050326
40689CB00008B/1254